NATHANIEL BACON

Virginia is one of England's biggest and wealthiest colonies in North America in 1675. But tensions are growing between the **rich planters** who own **large plantations** in the east and the **small farmers** that must go west into the **wooded frontier** to find land for themselves. That tension becomes **America's first open rebellion against England's royal power** when Nathaniel Bacon comes from England and takes up the small farmers' cause . . .

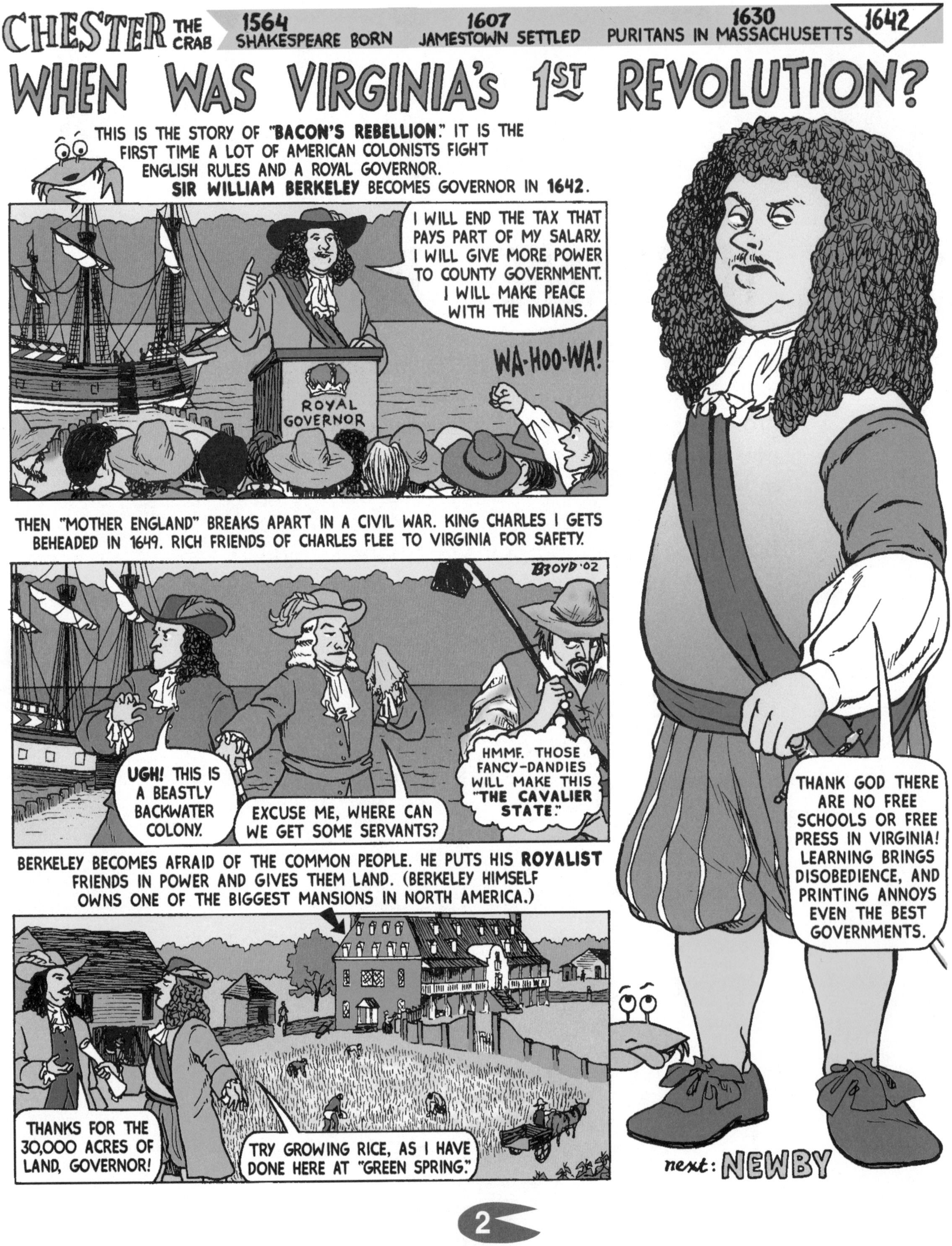
CHESTER THE CRAB
1564 SHAKESPEARE BORN
1607 JAMESTOWN SETTLED
1630 PURITANS IN MASSACHUSETTS
1642
WHEN WAS VIRGINIA'S 1ST REVOLUTION?
THIS IS THE STORY OF "BACON'S REBELLION." IT IS THE FIRST TIME A LOT OF AMERICAN COLONISTS FIGHT ENGLISH RULES AND A ROYAL GOVERNOR. SIR WILLIAM BERKELEY BECOMES GOVERNOR IN 1642.
I WILL END THE TAX THAT PAYS PART OF MY SALARY. I WILL GIVE MORE POWER TO COUNTY GOVERNMENT. I WILL MAKE PEACE WITH THE INDIANS.
ROYAL GOVERNOR
WA-HOO-WA!
THEN "MOTHER ENGLAND" BREAKS APART IN A CIVIL WAR. KING CHARLES I GETS BEHEADED IN 1649. RICH FRIENDS OF CHARLES FLEE TO VIRGINIA FOR SAFETY.
BOYD '02
UGH! THIS IS A BEASTLY BACKWATER COLONY.
EXCUSE ME, WHERE CAN WE GET SOME SERVANTS?
HMMF. THOSE FANCY-DANDIES WILL MAKE THIS "THE CAVALIER STATE."
BERKELEY BECOMES AFRAID OF THE COMMON PEOPLE. HE PUTS HIS ROYALIST FRIENDS IN POWER AND GIVES THEM LAND. (BERKELEY HIMSELF OWNS ONE OF THE BIGGEST MANSIONS IN NORTH AMERICA.)
THANKS FOR THE 30,000 ACRES OF LAND, GOVERNOR!
TRY GROWING RICE, AS I HAVE DONE HERE AT "GREEN SPRING."
THANK GOD THERE ARE NO FREE SCHOOLS OR FREE PRESS IN VIRGINIA! LEARNING BRINGS DISOBEDIENCE, AND PRINTING ANNOYS EVEN THE BEST GOVERNMENTS.
next: NEWBY

WHO WAS NATHANIEL BACON?

THE VIRGINIA COLONY IS BATTERED BY HAILSTORMS AND FLOODS IN THE EARLY 1670s. DISEASE WIPES OUT HALF THE CATTLE IN THE COLONY IN 1673.

INTO THIS TROUBLE STEPS ENGLISH GENTLEMAN **NATHANIEL BACON** IN **1675**. HE IS WELCOMED BY HIS COUSIN, FRANCES CULPEPER, AND HER NEW HUSBAND, **ROYAL GOVERNOR SIR WILLIAM BERKELEY.**

BACON GETS 1,200 ACRES BESIDE THE JAMES RIVER, 40 MILES WEST OF JAMESTOWN. HE SOON LEARNS THAT POOR WHITES ON THE FRONTIER ARE UNHAPPY...

THE RICH SPONGES HAVE SUCKED UP PUBLIC MONEY—TAKEN IT TO REPAIR THEIR TOTTERING FORTUNES. THE POOR PEOPLE OF THIS COLONY SHOULD BE CAREFUL!

next: PULLED PORK

WHY DID SETTLERS FIGHT INDIANS IN 1675?

THE VIRGINIA COLONY IN 1675...

Eat MoR Chicken

AHHH! ANOTHER SETTLER'S HOG EATING OUR BEANS! WE'LL TEACH THE CARELESS ENGLISH A LESSON!

DOEG INDIANS RAID THE NORTHERN VIRGINIA FARM OF THOMAS MATHEWS.

HEY! DON'T TAKE OUR ARRKG!

COLONISTS FIRE BACK, KILLING 24 INDIANS.

UMM, IS THIS VILLAGE THE DOEG TRIBE OR THE SUSQUEHANNOCK?

WHO CARES?!

THE SUSQUEHANNOCKS GET MAD. THEY GO TO WAR ON THE FRONTIER, KILLING DOZENS. IN MARCH 1676 THEY KILL TWO OF NATHANIEL BACON'S PLANTATION WORKERS.

GOVERNOR WILLIAM BERKELEY SHOULD GIVE ME PERMISSION TO LEAD YOU POOR FARMERS AGAINST THE TRIBES!

BERKELEY REFUSES TO GIVE BACON PERMISSION TO FIGHT THE INDIANS.

THESE SETTLERS ARE RABBLE!

IN 1646 I MADE TREATY WITH THE INDIANS, TRADING MY PROTECTION FOR DEERSKINS. NO ONE ATTACKS THEM UNLESS I SAY SO.

NOW THE BATTLE IS ABOUT WHO WILL CONTROL THE COLONY: BERKELEY AND HIS RICH BUDS OR THE POOR WHITES WHO JOIN BACON AT JORDAN'S POINT ON THE SOUTH SIDE OF THE JAMES RIVER.

FRIENDS! THE ROYAL GOVERNMENT IN JAMESTOWN IS UNJUST! ITS LAWS ARE WICKED!

next: Bring Home the BA-CON! BA-CON! BA-CON!

CHESTER THE CRAB 1607 JAMESTOWN SETTLED 1630 PURITANS IN MASSACHUSETTS 1663 CAROLINAS CHARTERED 1676

WHO RULED JAMESTOWN IN 1676?

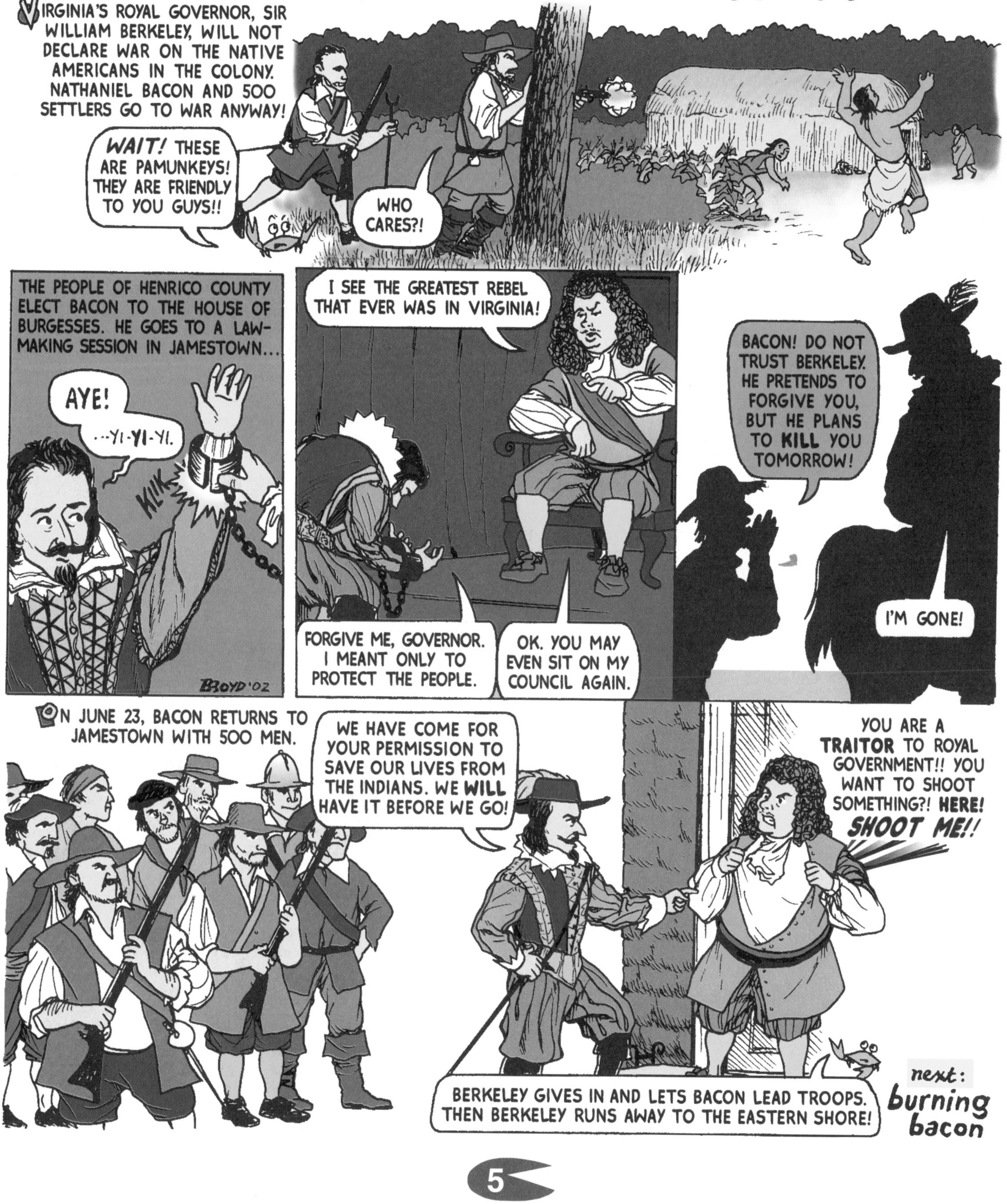

VIRGINIA'S ROYAL GOVERNOR, SIR WILLIAM BERKELEY, WILL NOT DECLARE WAR ON THE NATIVE AMERICANS IN THE COLONY. NATHANIEL BACON AND 500 SETTLERS GO TO WAR ANYWAY!
WAIT! THESE ARE PAMUNKEYS! THEY ARE FRIENDLY TO YOU GUYS!!
WHO CARES?!
THE PEOPLE OF HENRICO COUNTY ELECT BACON TO THE HOUSE OF BURGESSES. HE GOES TO A LAW-MAKING SESSION IN JAMESTOWN...
AYE!
...YI-YI-YI.
KLIK
BROYD '02
I SEE THE GREATEST REBEL THAT EVER WAS IN VIRGINIA!
FORGIVE ME, GOVERNOR. I MEANT ONLY TO PROTECT THE PEOPLE.
OK. YOU MAY EVEN SIT ON MY COUNCIL AGAIN.
BACON! DO NOT TRUST BERKELEY. HE PRETENDS TO FORGIVE YOU, BUT HE PLANS TO KILL YOU TOMORROW!
I'M GONE!
ON JUNE 23, BACON RETURNS TO JAMESTOWN WITH 500 MEN.
WE HAVE COME FOR YOUR PERMISSION TO SAVE OUR LIVES FROM THE INDIANS. WE WILL HAVE IT BEFORE WE GO!
YOU ARE A TRAITOR TO ROYAL GOVERNMENT!! YOU WANT TO SHOOT SOMETHING?! HERE! SHOOT ME!!
BERKELEY GIVES IN AND LETS BACON LEAD TROOPS. THEN BERKELEY RUNS AWAY TO THE EASTERN SHORE!
next: burning bacon

WHO WON BACON'S REBELLION?

ON SEPTEMBER **1676**, **NATHANIEL BACON** IS ATTACKING INDIANS ON VIRGINIA'S FRONTIER. HIS FOLLOWERS ARE TRYING TO CREATE A MORE DEMOCRATIC GOVERNMENT AT **JAMESTOWN**.

LOOK OUT! GOVERNOR BERKELEY IS COMING BACK WITH 600 TROOPS!

RUN AWAY!

BERKELEY'S VICTORY IS SHORT. BACON RETAKES JAMESTOWN BY USING THE WIVES OF BERKELEY'S MEN AS HOSTAGES.

THE GOVERNOR'S MEN WON'T FIRE BACK NOW!!

VOOM

BACON THEN ENDS THE DEBATE OVER WHO CONTROLS THE TOWN BY BURNING IT TO A CRISP.

BACON GETS SICK AND DIES IN OCTOBER. BERKELEY CAPTURES THE REBELLION'S NEW LEADER, JOSEPH INGRAM.

NATHANIEL BACON 1647 ~ 1676

BERKELEY TAKES CONTROL OF THE COLONY AGAIN. HE HANGS MORE THAN 14 REBELS AND TAKES THEIR PROPERTY FOR HIMSELF.

KING CHARLES II SENDS 1,000 ENGLISH SOLDIERS TO RESTORE ORDER.

THE KING ALSO WANTS **YOU** BACK IN **ENGLAND**, GOVERNOR!

BERKELEY DIES A FEW WEEKS LATER. BACON'S REBELLION LEAVES A MARK ON VIRGINIA:

USE OF BLACK SLAVES INCREASES (RICH WHITES THINK WHITE SERVANTS ARE TOO HARD TO CONTROL). END

CHAPTER 2

PATRICK HENRY

In 1699 the capital of Virginia moves from Jamestown to Williamsburg. There is calm for 60 years. But **Patrick Henry** is part of a generation of Virginians who are born on the frontier and grow up questioning the relationship their colony has to Mother England. Henry himself is bold enough to say these questions out loud, in public. He is in the colony's **House of Burgesses** only three days before he makes a ruckus by opposing the king's **Stamp Act** tax in **1765**. And the words only get hotter from there . . .

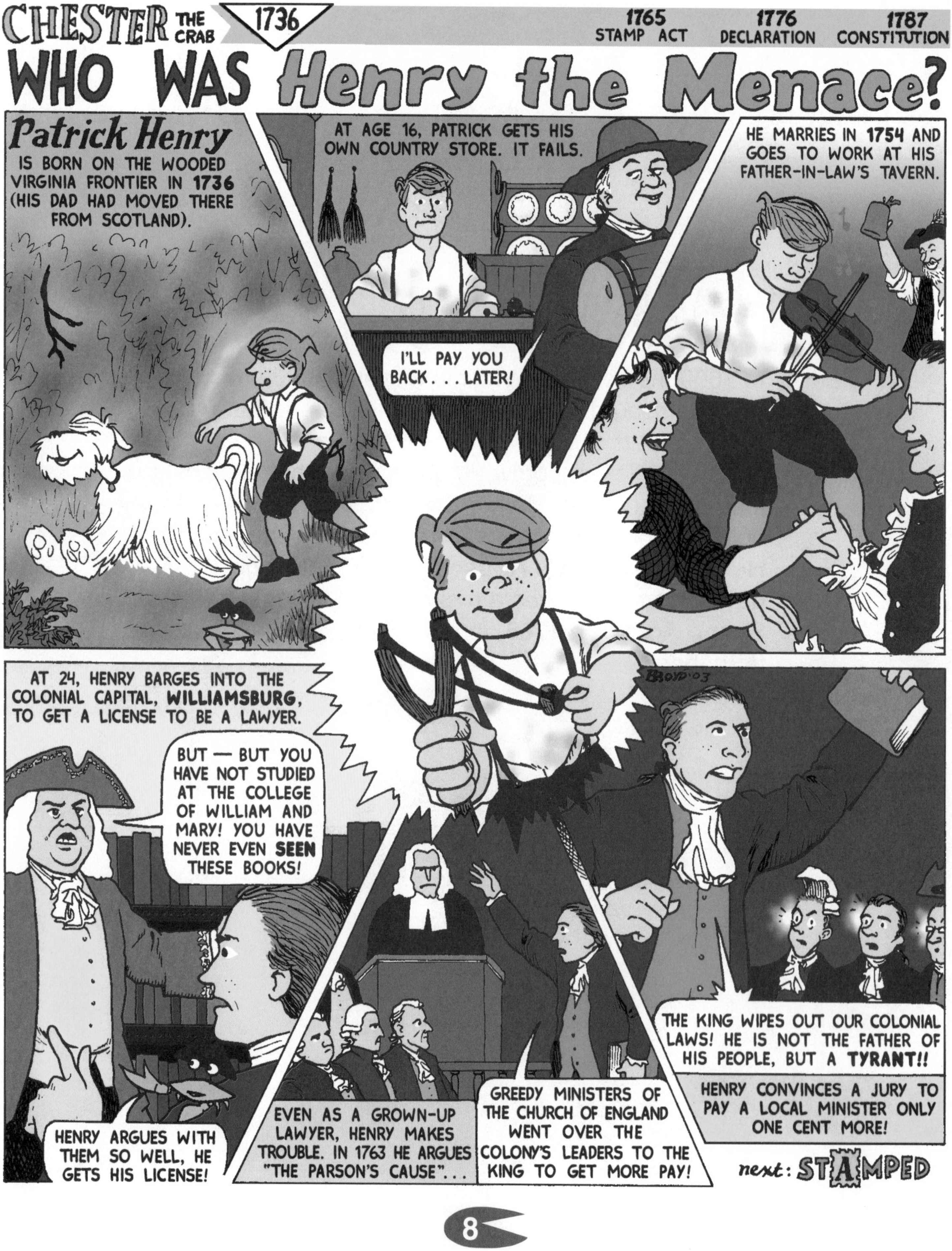
CHESTER THE CRAB
1736
1765 STAMP ACT
1776 DECLARATION
1787 CONSTITUTION
WHO WAS Henry the Menace?
Patrick Henry IS BORN ON THE WOODED VIRGINIA FRONTIER IN 1736 (HIS DAD HAD MOVED THERE FROM SCOTLAND).
AT AGE 16, PATRICK GETS HIS OWN COUNTRY STORE. IT FAILS.
I'LL PAY YOU BACK. . . LATER!
HE MARRIES IN 1754 AND GOES TO WORK AT HIS FATHER-IN-LAW'S TAVERN.
AT 24, HENRY BARGES INTO THE COLONIAL CAPITAL, WILLIAMSBURG, TO GET A LICENSE TO BE A LAWYER.
BUT — BUT YOU HAVE NOT STUDIED AT THE COLLEGE OF WILLIAM AND MARY! YOU HAVE NEVER EVEN SEEN THESE BOOKS!
HENRY ARGUES WITH THEM SO WELL, HE GETS HIS LICENSE!
EVEN AS A GROWN-UP LAWYER, HENRY MAKES TROUBLE. IN 1763 HE ARGUES "THE PARSON'S CAUSE"...
GREEDY MINISTERS OF THE CHURCH OF ENGLAND WENT OVER THE COLONY'S LEADERS TO THE KING TO GET MORE PAY!
THE KING WIPES OUT OUR COLONIAL LAWS! HE IS NOT THE FATHER OF HIS PEOPLE, BUT A TYRANT!!
HENRY CONVINCES A JURY TO PAY A LOCAL MINISTER ONLY ONE CENT MORE!
BBOYD·03
next: STAMPED

WHO FOUGHT THE KING'S STAMP TAX?

IN COLONIAL AMERICA, PEOPLE USUALLY **TRADE** FOR THINGS BECAUSE COINS AND PAPER MONEY ARE **SCARCE** (HARD TO FIND).

I'LL TRADE YOU A RED-EYES WHITE DRAGON CARD FOR YOUR CANE.

WHAT A **BARTER!**

THIS IS WHY COLONISTS GET MAD AT KING GEORGE III'S **STAMP ACT** IN **1765**. COLONISTS DON'T HAVE CASH TO PAY THIS TAX.

TO PAY ME FOR PROTECTING AMERICA IN THE WAR AGAINST THE **FRENCH AND INDIANS**, COLONISTS MUST PAY FOR AN OFFICIAL STAMP ON:

NEWSPAPERS | CALENDARS | LEGAL PAPERS | PLAYING CARDS | DICE | OVERSEAS TOBACCO SHIPMENTS

THIS ALLOWS THE KING TO CONTROL INFORMATION. IT'S ALSO THE FIRST TIME HE DIRECTLY TAXES HIS AMERICAN COLONIES.

IN MAY **1765**, THE RICH PLANTER JOHN ROBINSON IS LEADER OF **VIRGINIA'S HOUSE OF BURGESSES.**

THWAP!

Wha?!..WHO SHOT THAT SPITWAD?!!

ME — **PATRICK HENRY!** I HAVE BEEN A BURGESS FOR THREE DAYS NOW, BUT I HAVE SOME RESOLUTIONS AGAINST THE KING'S STAMP ACT.

BOYD '03

TREASON

IF THIS BE TREASON, **MAKE THE MOST OF IT!**

THE BURGESSES PASS MOST OF HENRY'S RESOLUTIONS. OTHER COLONIES COPY HENRY'S BOLD PROTEST.

WE SHOULD NOT BE TAXED BY ENGLAND IF WE HAVE **NO** AMERICAN IN ENGLAND TO VOTE ON THE TAX!

NO TAXATION WITHOUT REPRESENTATION!

ENGLAND REMOVES THE STAMP TAX!

next: **LIBERTY VS. DEATH**

HOW DID HENRY MENACE KING GEORGE?

THE AMERICAN COLONIES CONTINUE TO FIGHT WITH ENGLAND'S **KING GEORGE III** ABOUT **TAXES.**

IN **1775** VIRGINIA'S ROYAL GOVERNOR CALLS A BRITISH WARSHIP TO THE YORK RIVER. ONBOARD, THE GOV SAYS:

I AM THE BOSS OF VIRGINIA!

ELECTED MEMBERS OF VIRGINIA'S HOUSE OF BURGESSES MEET AT ST. JOHN'S CHURCH IN RICHMOND.

WE ARE THE BOSSES OF VIRGINIA!!

RESPECT FOR MOTHER ENGLAND

ROWDY BURGESS **PATRICK HENRY** SAYS:

THAT WARSHIP IS SENT HERE TO BIND US IN CHAINS — CHAINS THE BRITISH HAVE BEEN MAKING FOR US FOR **YEARS!!**

THE CHAINS' CLANKING MAY BE HEARD IN **BOSTON. WAR IS COMING!**

LET IT COME!!

IS LIFE SO DEAR OR **PEACE** SO SWEET AS TO BE BOUGHT AT THE PRICE OF CHAINS AND **SLAVERY?!!**

I KNOW NOT WHAT CHOICE **OTHERS** MAY MAKE...

BUT AS FOR ME, **GIVE ME LIBERTY** OR GIVE ME **DEATH!**

SHOW ME THE LIBERTY!!

THREE WEEKS LATER, GOVERNOR DUNMORE MAKES BRITISH SOLDIERS TAKE GUNPOWDER FROM WILLIAMSBURG'S MAGAZINE TO HIS WARSHIP. HENRY LEADS COLONISTS TO GET IT BACK! DUNMORE REFUSES — BUT PAYS FOR THE POWDER.

next: The Gov Goes

WHO WAS VIRGINIA'S 1ST ELECTED GOVERNOR?

VIRGINIANS HAVE MADE AN UNEASY PEACE WITH THEIR ROYAL GOVERNOR IN **APRIL 1775.** THEN...

FIGHTING IN MASSACHUSETTS! REDCOATS AND COLONISTS HAVE FIRED "THE SHOT HEARD 'ROUND THE WORLD!!"

TIME TO VISIT THE GOVERNOR'S PALACE!!

÷AHEM÷ I BELIEVE IT'S TIME TO **LEAVE** THE GOVERNOR'S PALACE.

HEY, LORD DUNMORE IS GONE!

HMMM. I WOULD LIKE TO LIVE HERE!

A YEAR LATER, HENRY AND OTHERS WRITE A PLAN FOR A NEW VIRGINIA GOVERNMENT. THIS ONE USES **DEMOCRATIC** IDEAS AND PROTECTS **INDIVIDUAL RIGHTS!**

Commonwealth of VIRGINIA Constitution

LET'S ELECT GOVERNORS TO ONE-YEAR TERMS. LET'S MAKE PATRICK HENRY OUR **FIRST ELECTED GOVERNOR**...

BOYD '03

Dear Fellow Patriots GO FOR IT!

THANKS. WE VIRGINIANS HAVE DECLARED OUR INDEPENDENCE FROM ENGLAND. NOW WE URGE THE SECOND CONTINENTAL CONGRESS IN PHILADELPHIA TO DO THE SAME!

CONGRESS PASSES ITS **DECLARATION OF INDEPENDENCE** ON **JULY 4, 1776.**

TWO DAYS LATER, HENRY BEGINS HIS GOVERNORSHIP. HE SERVES SEVERAL TERMS (1776-79 AND 1784-86).

next: Constitutional Matters

WHY DID HENRY MENACE THE CONSTITUTION?

NEAR THE END OF HIS LIFE, ROWDY **PATRICK HENRY** PICKS ONE MORE FIGHT...

The Constitution
We the People

FIGHT? ISN'T HENRY A "FOUNDING FATHER?"

HENRY'S FIRE HELPED LIGHT THE AMERICAN REVOLUTION. **NOW** HE WORRIES THAT HIS FOUNDING BUDDIES ARE MAKING A GOVERNMENT AS POWERFUL AS THE ENGLISH ONE THEY ESCAPED!

THIS CONSTITUTION ALLOWS CONGRESS TO TAX VIRGINIA EVEN IF WE DISAGREE! IT IS "TAXATION WITHOUT REPRESENTATION" ALL OVER AGAIN!!

PATRICK HENRY

VIRGINIAN JAMES MADISON "FATHER OF THE CONSTITUTION"

EACH STATE IS REPRESENTED! MAJORITY RULES. WHY, OUR OWN VIRGINIA GENERAL ASSEMBLY TAXES COUNTIES EVEN IF THEY OPPOSE A STATE TAX!

WE DON'T NEED SUCH A POWERFUL CENTRAL GOVERNMENT. OUR RIGHT TO TRAVEL THE **MISSISSIPPI RIVER** IS GUARANTEED BY OUR TREATIES, FOR EXAMPLE.

YOU WOULD RATHER HAVE OTHER NATIONS PROTECT YOUR RIGHTS THAN YOUR FELLOW AMERICANS?! OUR GOVERNMENT UNDER THE CONSTITUTION WOULD BE BETTER THAN THE ARTICLES OF CONFEDERATION AT DEFENDING THE MISSISSIPPI.

HUMPF! WE HAVE A BILL OF RIGHTS IN VIRGINIA TO PROTECT OUR INDIVIDUAL RIGHTS FROM THE STATE GOVERNMENT. IN THIS NATIONAL CONSTITUTION, WE LEAVE OURSELVES OPEN TO THE ARMED AND THE POWERFUL!

Bill of Rights

OTHER STATES ALSO WANT A NATIONAL BILL OF RIGHTS. PASS THIS CONSTITUTION AND THE NEW GOVERNMENT WILL ADD ONE TO IT!

VIRGINIA RATIFIES THE CONSTITUTION IN 1788. THE **BILL OF RIGHTS** IS ADDED IN **1791**.

HENRY DIES IN **1799**, BUT HIS WORDS CONTINUE TO RING LOUDLY IN OUR NATIONAL DEBATES!

ALWAYS BE WATCHFUL OF YOUR LIBERTY!! END

GEORGE WASHINGTON

Young George Washington surveys the frontier to mark off land for settlers, and he wants to join the British army. But the **Redcoats** will not have him. So he is available in 1775 when the rebelling American colonies need a general to lead their patriot soldiers. Washington holds the ragtag troops together until his **victory at Yorktown in 1781** smashes a major British force. Winning a war against the world's superpower is amazing enough. But now Washington will face an even bigger challenge: forming a peacetime government that will hold the American states together . . .

WHY DID AMERICA NEED A PRESIDENT?

OK, CHRISTIE, TEST REVIEW! WHAT DO YOU KNOW ABOUT **GEORGE WASHINGTON**?

UMM. HE WAS "FATHER OF OUR COUNTRY." HE WAS COMMANDER-IN-CHIEF DURING THE AMERICAN REVOLUTION. HE WAS THE FIRST PRESIDENT. HE'S WORTH 25 CENTS.

BOYD '01

GREAT! BUT DO YOU KNOW **HOW** HE BECAME PRESIDENT? OR HOW **HARD** IT WAS TO BE THE FIRST PRESIDENT OF THE UNITED STATES?

NO.

LET'S LEARN! AFTER THE REVOLUTION, WASHINGTON GIVES HIS SWORD TO CONGRESS AND RETURNS TO **MOUNT VERNON**, HIS FARM IN **VIRGINIA**. HE WANTS TO BE LEFT ALONE NOW.

THE NEW COUNTRY IS REALLY JUST A LOOSE COLLECTION OF 13 STATES. "**THE ARTICLES OF CONFEDERATION**" ALLOW ONLY A WEAK CENTRAL GOVERNMENT.

TAXES?! I'M NOT GIVING **OUR** STATE MONEY TO CONGRESS!

WHO IS IN CHARGE HERE??

ALL OF US!

THE NATION NEEDS WASHINGTON AGAIN. IN **1787** HE GETS DRAGGED TO PHILADELPHIA WITH LEADERS FROM OTHER STATES.

LET'S TRY A **CONSTITUTION**. WE GET A STRONGER CENTRAL GOVERNMENT, BUT THE POWER WILL **BALANCE** BETWEEN THREE BRANCHES.

VIRGINIAN JAMES MADISON

"PRESIDENT" — EXECUTIVE BRANCH

VS.

VS.

"CONGRESS" — LEGISLATIVE BRANCH

VS.

"SUPREME COURT" — JUDICIAL BRANCH

WE ALREADY HAVE A CONGRESS TO PASS LAWS. WE NEED A "PRESIDENT" TO ENFORCE THEM.

NOOOW, WHO COULD **THAT** BE, HMMMM?

NICE POWER POINT PRESENTATION!

next: **ELECTION**

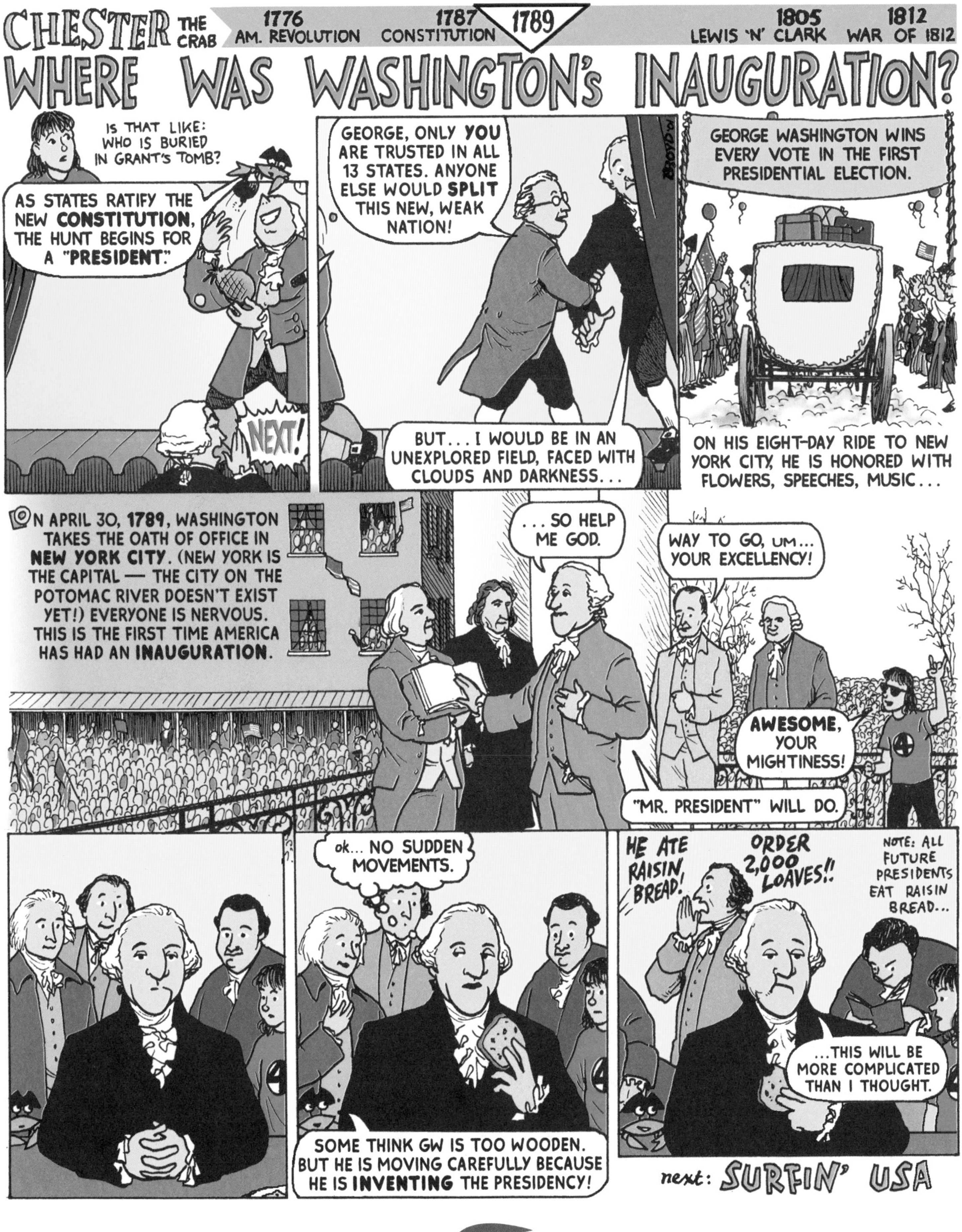
CHESTER THE CRAB
1776 AM. REVOLUTION
1787 CONSTITUTION
1789
1805 LEWIS 'N' CLARK
1812 WAR OF 1812
WHERE WAS WASHINGTON's INAUGURATION?
IS THAT LIKE: WHO IS BURIED IN GRANT'S TOMB?
AS STATES RATIFY THE NEW CONSTITUTION, THE HUNT BEGINS FOR A "PRESIDENT."
NEXT!
GEORGE, ONLY YOU ARE TRUSTED IN ALL 13 STATES. ANYONE ELSE WOULD SPLIT THIS NEW, WEAK NATION!
BUT... I WOULD BE IN AN UNEXPLORED FIELD, FACED WITH CLOUDS AND DARKNESS...
GEORGE WASHINGTON WINS EVERY VOTE IN THE FIRST PRESIDENTIAL ELECTION.
ON HIS EIGHT-DAY RIDE TO NEW YORK CITY, HE IS HONORED WITH FLOWERS, SPEECHES, MUSIC...
ON APRIL 30, 1789, WASHINGTON TAKES THE OATH OF OFFICE IN NEW YORK CITY. (NEW YORK IS THE CAPITAL — THE CITY ON THE POTOMAC RIVER DOESN'T EXIST YET!) EVERYONE IS NERVOUS. THIS IS THE FIRST TIME AMERICA HAS HAD AN INAUGURATION.
...SO HELP ME GOD.
WAY TO GO, UM... YOUR EXCELLENCY!
AWESOME, YOUR MIGHTINESS!
"MR. PRESIDENT" WILL DO.
ok... NO SUDDEN MOVEMENTS.
SOME THINK GW IS TOO WOODEN. BUT HE IS MOVING CAREFULLY BECAUSE HE IS INVENTING THE PRESIDENCY!
HE ATE RAISIN BREAD!
ORDER 2,000 LOAVES!!
NOTE: ALL FUTURE PRESIDENTS EAT RAISIN BREAD...
...THIS WILL BE MORE COMPLICATED THAN I THOUGHT.
next: SURFIN' USA

WHAT IS IN WASHINGTON'S FIRST TERM?

HOW DID WASHINGTON VIEW THE WORLD?

THE FIRST TERM OF THE FIRST PRESIDENT OF THE UNITED STATES IS OVER IN 1792. **GEORGE WASHINGTON** REALLY WANTS TO GO HOME.

FEDERALIST ALEXANDER HAMILTON

BUT I STAY TO KEEP THESE TWO GUYS FROM KILLING EACH OTHER — OR THE NATION!

DEMOCRATIC-REPUBLICAN THOMAS JEFFERSON

BRITAIN IS BETTER!

Vive La France!

THINGS ARE CRAZY ENOUGH AT HOME THAT WASHINGTON TRIES TO KEEP AMERICA OUT OF THE WORLD'S AFFAIRS.

U.S.

WE'LL HAVE NO ENTANGLING ALLIANCES.

FRANCE HAS HAD ITS OWN REVOLUTION (IN 1789). IN **1792**, FRANCE DECLARES ITSELF A **REPUBLIC**, JUST LIKE AMERICA. THEN FRANCE DECLARES WAR ON BRITAIN.

COPYCATS!

T.J.

NOW, WILL AMERICA HELP FRANCE THE WAY FRANCE HELPED **US** WIN **OUR** FREEDOM?

WASHINGTON KNOWS AMERICA IS TOO WEAK TO GO TO WAR AGAIN. HE AGREES TO AT LEAST HONOR REPUBLICAN FRANCE BY MEETING WITH ITS AMBASSADOR.

EDMOND GENÉT ARRIVES IN SOUTH CAROLINA IN **1793**. HE BEGINS A TOUR OF THE EAST COAST. JEFFERSONIAN REPUBLICANS LOVE HIM.

GENET

LIBERTY! EQUALITY! FRATERNITY!

HAMILTON AND THE FEDERALISTS DO **NOT**.

LOUIS XVI

THE FRENCH REVOLUTION HAS GONE TOO FAR! THEY KILLED THE KING WHO HELPED US IN 1781!

WASHINGTON SAYS AMERICA WILL **NOT** HELP FRANCE **OR** BRITAIN. THIS DOES NOT SLOW DOWN GENÉT.

BOYD '01

GW IS A FEEBLE FOOL! I'LL PAY FOR THESE AMERICAN SHIPS TO GO ATTACK THE BRITISH.

HEY! OUR **PRESIDENT** IS THE GUY WHO LEADS US INTO WAR. GET LOST, BUSTER!

next: ANOTHER TAX WAR

WHO ENDED THE WHISKEY REBELLION?

IN THE BATTLE OF THE FEDERALISTS **VS.** THE DEMOCRAT-REPUBLICANS, FEDERALIST ALEXANDER HAMILTON SAYS:

THE NEW **CONSTITUTION** GIVES THE FEDERAL GOVERNMENT THE RIGHT TO **TAX.** LET'S TAX!!

HAMILTON GETS AN **EXCISE TAX** — A TAX ON ONE SPECIFIC PRODUCT...

WHISKEY, A STRONG DRINK MADE FROM GRAIN.

SETTLERS WEST OF THE APPALACHIAN MOUNTAINS GET UPSET. THEY WILL NOT PAY A TAX ON SOMETHING THEY MAKE THEMSELVES **FOR** THEMSELVES.

EASTERNERS ARE STEALING OUR MONEY!

FEDERAL TAX COLLECTORS ARE ATTACKED IN WESTERN PENNSYLVANIA.

WE HAVE TO OBEY ONLY OUR **LOCAL** GOVERNMENT. THE CONSTITUTION SAYS SO.

TAR

FEATHER

Federal Treasury

MR. PRESIDENT, THE REBELS THREATEN THE ENTIRE NATION. WE MUST BE ABLE TO RAISE MONEY! THE CONSTITUTION SAYS SO!

THIS IS THE FIRST BIG TEST FOR THE FEDERAL GOVERNMENT. CAN IT ENFORCE ITS OWN LAWS??

WASHINGTON PUTS HIS MILITARY UNIFORM ON AGAIN. HE CALLS FOR 13,000 MILITIAMEN TO END "**THE WHISKEY REBELLION**" IN 1794.

:Sigh: HERE WE GO AGAIN.

HIS FORCE ARRESTS 150 PENNSYLVANIANS. TWO ARE CONDEMNED TO DIE, BUT WASHINGTON PARDONS THEM. THE REBELLION IS OVER.

AMERICA IS FINALLY STRONG ENOUGH TO GO ON WITHOUT ME.

GW LEAVES THE PRESIDENCY IN **1797.** HE DIES JUST TWO YEARS LATER. **END**

JOHN MARSHALL

In 1801, America has a working government and some stability after George Washington's two terms as president. But the job of founding (forming) America is not done yet. One of the nation's **three government branches** is still very weak: the **judiciary**. There is not true balance in our **system of checks and balances**. Virginian John Marshall is put on the **United States Supreme Court** in 1801 -- can he do something to build the power of judges?

HOW DID JOHN MARSHALL START JUDGING?

CHUNK

BROYD '00

PAFF

CHESTER, **WHAT** ARE YOU DOING?!

THROWING QUOITS!

QUOITS? THAT'S A NEW JUNGLE POKEMON, I THINK.

IT'S LIKE HORSESHOES. IT IS A POPULAR GAME IN THE 1700s — ESPECIALLY WITH ONE VIRGINIAN:

JOHN MARSHALL

WHEN WAR AGAINST ENGLAND BEGINS, MARSHALL JOINS **GEORGE WASHINGTON'S** ARMY JUST IN TIME FOR ITS HARD WINTER AT **VALLEY FORGE** IN PENNSYLVANIA.

TH--THIS IS F-F-FUN, JOHN, B-BUT I WOULD RATHER EAT. WHY WON'T OUR STATES SEND FOOD?

EACH STATE LOOKS OUT FOR ITSELF. NO ONE WANTS TO GIVE UP POWER TO A CENTRAL AUTHORITY — NOT EVEN TO GENERAL WASHINGTON. HE MUST BEG STATES TO SEND US FOOD, GUNS...

HA! I WON, CHARLIE!!

NO, I WON!

TRUST A DEPUTY JUDGE ADVOCATE OF THE ARMY TO SETTLE THIS! BASED ON THE EVIDENCE, JOE WINS!

MARSHALL STUDIES LAW AT THE COLLEGE OF WILLIAM AND MARY IN VIRGINIA.

TODAY WE STUDY ELECTION LAW...

PROFESSOR GEORGE WYTHE

HE DOES NOT STUDY LONG.

YOU'RE LEAVING AFTER A FEW WEEKS?!!

SORRY! MET A CUTE GIRL.

next: THE SHIELD

WHERE ARE COURTS IN THE CONSTITUTION?

JOHN MARSHALL HAS LITTLE LAW SCHOOL TRAINING. STILL, HE READS ENOUGH TO GET A LAW LICENSE IN **1780** FROM VIRGINIA GOVERNOR **THOMAS JEFFERSON.**

THE REVOLUTION ENDS IN 1783. LAWS ARE A MESS.

THE NATIONAL GOVERNMENT WANTS FARMERS TO PAY THEIR DEBTS TO ENGLISH STORES. **WE** IN THE GENERAL ASSEMBLY WILL PROTECT POOR FARMERS BY PASSING LAWS TO DELAY PAYMENTS!

THE STATES DO NOT COOPERATE UNDER THE **ARTICLES OF CONFEDERATION**. IN 1787, A **CONSTITUTION** IS WRITTEN. IT WILL MAKE A NEW GOVERNMENT IF 9 OF THE 13 STATES AGREE.

SOUTH CAROLINA IS THE EIGHTH STATE TO APPROVE!

MAYBE VIRGINIA WILL BE "LOVE PETITION NO. 9."

STOP TOSSING QUOITS! DEBATE IS STARTING!

PATRICK HENRY SAYS:

A **FEDERAL** GOVERNMENT WILL BE TOO STRONG! ITS TAX AGENTS WILL TRASH EVERY BARN AND HOUSE LOOKING FOR MONEY!

GEORGE WYTHE SAYS:

WE WILL ELECT **REPRESENTATIVES** TO THE NATIONAL GOVERNMENT. THEY WILL CONTROL TAXES.

WHAT ABOUT THE PLAN'S **NATIONAL COURT SYSTEM**?! VIRGINIANS WILL BE DRAGGED TO A FARAWAY CITY FOR TRIAL! THEY WON'T BE JUDGED BY THEIR NEIGHBORS!

MARSHALL SAYS:

STATES WILL STILL HAVE COURTS FOR **LOCAL** DISPUTES.

WE NEED A NATIONAL COURT TO PROTECT INDIVIDUAL FREEDOMS ACROSS THE WHOLE COUNTRY. THE COURT CAN BE A **SHIELD** TO KEEP CONGRESS OR A PRESIDENT FROM GETTING TOO POWERFUL.

AS VIRGINIANS DEBATE, NEW HAMPSHIRE BECOMES THE IMPORTANT NINTH STATE TO APPROVE THE CONSTITUTION. VIRGINIA SAYS YES IN 1788!

next: THE CHIEF

HOW STRONG WAS THE SUPREME COURT?

JOHN MARSHALL, YOU MUST LIKE THE **CONSTITUTION**.

I WOULD — IF IT DID WHAT IT IS SUPPOSED TO: BALANCE POWER BETWEEN THE BRANCHES OF OUR FEDERAL GOVERNMENT.

JUDICIAL BRANCH

EXECUTIVE BRANCH

LEGISLATIVE BRANCH

BOYD '00

IN THESE EARLY DAYS OF THE UNITED STATES, OUR SCALES OF POWER ARE UPENDED!

THE **JUDICIAL BRANCH** IS WEAK. FEDERAL JUDGES MAKE POLITICAL SPEECHES IN COURT TO SUPPORT THE PRESIDENT WHO GAVE THEM THEIR JOBS.

BUT THAT KIND OF SHIFTY POLITICS PUTS MARSHALL ON THE SUPREME COURT IN FEBRUARY 1801.

YES, PRESIDENT **ADAMS**?

I LOST THE ELECTION — I WILL BE PRESIDENT ONLY A FEW MORE DAYS. YOU MUST JOIN THE COURT SO OUR **FEDERALIST** IDEAS WILL STILL BE HEARD AFTER I GO.

THE NEW PRESIDENT WITH REPUBLICAN IDEAS WILL BE **THOMAS JEFFERSON**.

I DON'T TRUST THE WAY THE FEDERALISTS HELP **BUSINESSMEN**.

MARSHALL AND THE FEDERALIST JUDGES CAN SERVE THEIR WHOLE LIVES...

UNLESS I FIND A WAY TO IMPEACH THEM!!

DO YOU PROMISE TO UPHOLD THE CONSTITUTION AS PRESIDENT, TOM?

I DO.

YEAH, RIGHT.

YOU'RE GOING DOWN, JOHN-BOY!!!

next: LAW, ORDER

22

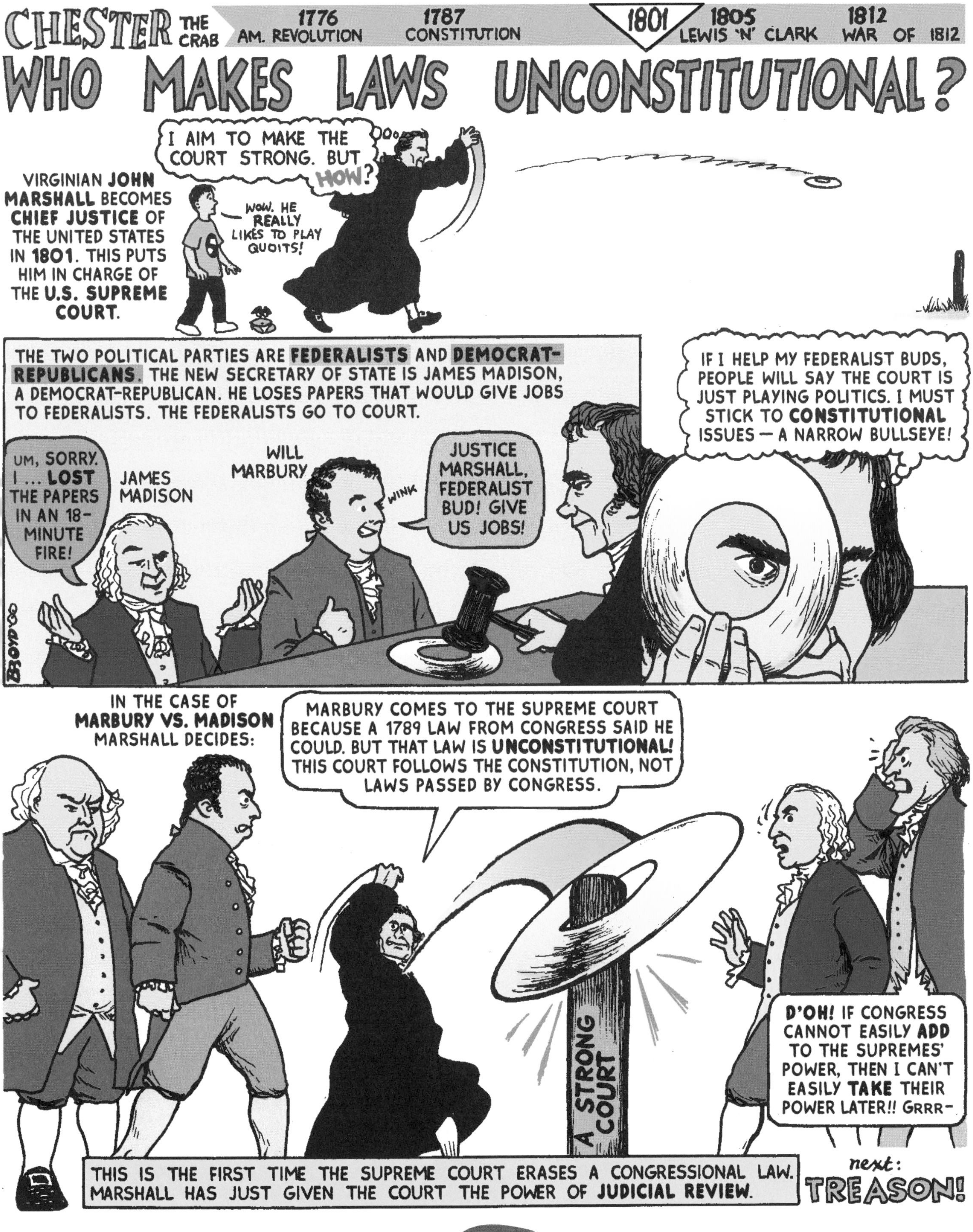

CHESTER THE CRAB
1776 AM. REVOLUTION
1787 CONSTITUTION
1801
1805 LEWIS 'N' CLARK
1812 WAR OF 1812
WHO MAKES LAWS UNCONSTITUTIONAL?
VIRGINIAN JOHN MARSHALL BECOMES CHIEF JUSTICE OF THE UNITED STATES IN 1801. THIS PUTS HIM IN CHARGE OF THE U.S. SUPREME COURT.
I AIM TO MAKE THE COURT STRONG. BUT HOW?
WOW. HE REALLY LIKES TO PLAY QUOITS!
THE TWO POLITICAL PARTIES ARE FEDERALISTS AND DEMOCRAT-REPUBLICANS. THE NEW SECRETARY OF STATE IS JAMES MADISON, A DEMOCRAT-REPUBLICAN. HE LOSES PAPERS THAT WOULD GIVE JOBS TO FEDERALISTS. THE FEDERALISTS GO TO COURT.
UM, SORRY. I ... LOST THE PAPERS IN AN 18-MINUTE FIRE!
JAMES MADISON
WILL MARBURY
WINK
JUSTICE MARSHALL, FEDERALIST BUD! GIVE US JOBS!
IF I HELP MY FEDERALIST BUDS, PEOPLE WILL SAY THE COURT IS JUST PLAYING POLITICS. I MUST STICK TO CONSTITUTIONAL ISSUES — A NARROW BULLSEYE!
BROYD '06
IN THE CASE OF MARBURY VS. MADISON MARSHALL DECIDES:
MARBURY COMES TO THE SUPREME COURT BECAUSE A 1789 LAW FROM CONGRESS SAID HE COULD. BUT THAT LAW IS UNCONSTITUTIONAL! THIS COURT FOLLOWS THE CONSTITUTION, NOT LAWS PASSED BY CONGRESS.
A STRONG COURT
D'OH! IF CONGRESS CANNOT EASILY ADD TO THE SUPREMES' POWER, THEN I CAN'T EASILY TAKE THEIR POWER LATER!! GRRR-
THIS IS THE FIRST TIME THE SUPREME COURT ERASES A CONGRESSIONAL LAW. MARSHALL HAS JUST GIVEN THE COURT THE POWER OF JUDICIAL REVIEW.
next: TREASON!

DID POLITICS OR THE LAW SAVE BURR?

PRESIDENT THOMAS JEFFERSON IS MAD AT U.S. CHIEF JUSTICE JOHN MARSHALL.

THAT FINK FEDERALIST! HE WON'T DO WHAT I WANT HIM TO DO.

SIR! AARON BURR JUST KILLED ALEXANDER HAMILTON IN A DUEL!

AARON BURR — WHO ALMOST BEAT ME FOR THE PRESIDENCY! HMMMM...

NEW JERSEY CHARGES BURR WITH MURDER. HE ESCAPES!

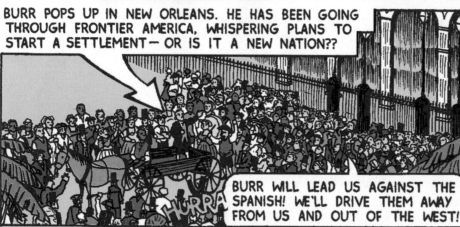

BURR POPS UP IN NEW ORLEANS. HE HAS BEEN GOING THROUGH FRONTIER AMERICA, WHISPERING PLANS TO START A SETTLEMENT — OR IS IT A NEW NATION??

HURRA

BURR WILL LEAD US AGAINST THE SPANISH! WE'LL DRIVE THEM AWAY FROM US AND OUT OF THE WEST!

BUT I AM TALKING WITH SPAIN ABOUT A PEACE TREATY! I WANT BURR ARRESTED FOR TREASON!!

JUSTICE MARSHALL! THE PRESIDENT WANTS BURR HANGED. IF YOU FREE BURR, YOU COULD BE IMPEACHED. WHAT NOW?

THE SUPREME COURT WILL NOT GRAB POWER — NOR WILL IT SHRINK FROM ITS DUTY. BRING IT ON!!

KINGS USE CHARGES OF TREASON TO KILL THEIR ENEMIES. IN AMERICA, WE FOLLOW THE LAW INSTEAD. THE CONSTITUTION SAYS "TREASON" IS AN ACT OF WAR AGAINST THE U.S. BURR MAY HAVE PLANNED A WAR, BUT HE DID NOT ACTUALLY START ONE.

NOT GUILTY

KLANG

MARSHALL PROTECTS THE SUPREME COURT FROM POLITICS DURING HIS 34 YEARS AS CHIEF JUSTICE. JUST AS GEORGE WASHINGTON SHOWED HOW A PRESIDENT SHOULD BEHAVE, MARSHALL SET THE EXAMPLE FOR SUPREME COURT JUSTICES! END